CW00341249

IMAGES
of England

AROUND
FRAMPTON COTTERELL
AND WINTERBOURNE

Memories of the Village Shop
Palmers in Winterbourne Down
1876-1992

It stood on the corner, so easy to reach,
Helpful for those with troubled feet,
Shelves were packed with goodies complete,
And a smile to greet you, a welcome treat,
It served the village for many a decade,
From Father to Son yes, Palmer's the name.

Our school days in the early teens,
Many memories to recall with esteem,
Its bakehouse aroma, fresh crusty bread,
Delivered to our homes to keep us fed,
There tasty Cheese, neatly cut with a wire,
A wholesome snack an welcome desire,
I'll remember that cheese of childhood,
The cottage loaf we cut with a knife,
Kids helped with errands and housework,
And men went to work, not the wife.

It was Gilbert then, on the Grocery side,
Florence, his wife, on the drapery would abide,
Her measure and scissors, firm in hand,
Cut lengths to order, so precise would stand,
Gilbert, to us kids, such a friendly fellow,
Keeping his patience, despite our bellows,
He sometimes would a tuneful ditty sing,
And challenge us kids to learn and bring,
The reward was tempting, sweets or cake,
What an effort was all would make.

It took much practice, I can assure,
Even in school class it was a lure,
When progress gradually did take shape,

Back to Gilbert, our efforts make.
Then standing shy at the counter with glee
The reward to receive, fruit cake for tea,
Names of character in this shop have been
So sad now, they have left the scene.

Us local kids and friends, whoever,
Made our fun for simple pleasure,
Now times have changes in our wake
For progress, if any, yet to make,
But days are all uncertain still,
Whichever way decides your will.

With no available money for flicks,
Just the usual Saturday kicks,
The simple games we plated in the Paddock,
Then ran home to the tasty Faggot,
Or Cheese which never needed and ice chest,
And bread, so crusty and hot,
Boys and Girls were seldom unhappy,
And Mothers content with their lot.

I'll remember long that cheese of childhood,
And the cottage loaf we cut with a knife,
We helped with errands and housework,
And men went to work, not the wife,
Yes, I remember the shop on the corner,
When a penn'orth of lollies was sold.
Do you think I'm a bit too nostalgic,
Or is it I'm just getting old?

IMAGES
of England

AROUND FRAMPTON COTTERELL AND WINTERBOURNE

Compiled by
Veronica Smith
Jeffrey Spittal
(Frampton Cotterell, Coalpit Heath)
Sydney Marks
(Watley's End, Winterbourne, Winterbourne Down)
Derek Andrews
(Coalpit Heath)

TEMPUS

First published 2000
Copyright © Veronica Smith et al, 2000

Tempus Publishing Limited
The Mill, Brimscombe Port,
Stroud, Gloucestershire, GL5 2QG

ISBN 0 7524 2050 X

Typesetting and origination by
Tempus Publishing Limited
Printed in Great Britain by
Midway Clark Printing, Wiltshire

This book is dedicated to Mrs Evelyn Spittal

The Hearle family in the garden of their bungalow 'Epworth' in School Road, Frampton Cotterell, in 1925. The young girl is their daily help, Gladys Cook. The boys are sons Antony (on the rocking horse) and Dennis (on the tricycle) both of whom grew up to follow noteworthy ministerial careers.

Contents

Acknowledgements

Mr M. Tozer, Miss E.M. Skinner, Mr J. Marshall, Mr J.B. White, Mr A. Harding, The Reverend D. Hearle, Mrs J. Parnell, Mrs Monica Prideaux, Mrs Marion Wren, Mr L. Bowyer, Mrs Connie Holbrook, Mr Ian Hadrell, Mr G Laundy, Mr D. Andrews, Mrs Maureen Thompson, Mr R. Crew, Mr W. Amos for photographs. To Random House; Penguin UK; Bristol Industrial Archaeological Society (BIAS) and Mrs P.L. Hopkins for use of published material. To Mrs Muriel Brittain (Jesus College, Cambridge) for information on p. 22 and Mrs Linda Hall for information on p. 33.

Every effort has been made to identify copyright holders of illustrations from published materials, but we apologize to anyone overlooked in our search, or to photograph owners, should their names be omitted from the above list.

Introduction

This book is a collaboration of a number of people and sources. Under the guidance of Veronica Smith and with the initial help of Jeffrey Spittal who then introduced Derek Andrews to the project, and not forgetting Syd Marks, the book charts the history of these communities in South Gloucestershire. The area is about four miles east to west and one and a half north to south lying between Yate and the outskirts of Bristol at Downend. There is a gradual overall ascent of little more than fifty feet from Coalpit Heath with its intermittent involvement in mining since the fourteenth century, through Frampton Cotterell – the oldest of our settlements and divided by the River Frome – to the Marle Hills just over 200ft high in the western part of the parish, their name affording a clue to the quality of those rich soils nurturing the string of market gardens formerly almost continuous to the limits of Stapleton and, according to a post war survey, of Gloucestershire – 'the second best arable land of the country'.

Now a favoured and generally expensive commuter residential area our villages have fortunately escaped the blanketing anonymous sprawl of either Yate or Bradley Stoke and amongst the newer developments some traces of the past are still discernable. The new residents have come to ask questions about the where and why of what they see. It is hoped that this book will do something to satisfy their awakened interest and encourage them to investigate further.

FRAMPTON COTTERELL

In the Domesday Book [1086] the name appears as 'Frantone' indicating a Saxon settlement already established 'by the Frome'. It is most likely that this settlement was on the high ridge of land extending from Upper Chapel Lane to Frampton End Road. 'Cotterell' refers to the Cotel family of French descent who were owners of Frampton Court (on the site of the present Court Farm) from the late eleventh century to the middle of the thirteenth century.

Later, with water power becoming of economic importance, there was development along the river itself. By the middle of the sixteenth century the great un-enclosed fields formerly sustaining local agriculture had become broken up into smaller areas and many small 'closes' though 'Frampton Common' (the area now bounded by School Road, Bristol Road and the western end of Church Road) retained the name on a local postbox in the 1970s. On the far side of the present Church Farm Estate lay the territory of Frampton Court covering an area between Watley's End Road, Park Lane from Step House to Harris Barton, Rockwell Wood and the rear garden limits of properties in School Road and Rectory Road.

Early industrial activities are evident from mentions of a coal mine as early as 1301 and again in 1676 and minor field names point to iron smelting in the sixteenth century. It was, however, only in the nineteenth century that these mineral resources came to be worked extensively within the parish or on its boundaries. Coal was mined from 1853 to 1949 at Frog Lane Pit and iron-ore was mined from 1862 to 1874 on land behind the present water works site off Church Road. From 1823 hatting became the dominant village industry with a large factory in Park Lane as well as other domestic workplaces elsewhere, successors in their trade to that of feltmakers who had moved from Bristol in the latter part of the seventeenth century. The 1841 census of Frampton Cotterell identified exactly 200 people as hatters. Nearly half of them worked in the three storey buildings in Park Lane where, between 1818 and 1823, a factory was erected by Messrs Christy of Bermondsey.

For about a hundred years from the 1770s the population expanded rapidly accounting for both a boom in Free Church worship and eventually the re-building and enlargement of the parish church. From just under 400 residents in 1776 the total rose to just under 2,100 in 1871 and the number of houses in the same period from 75 to 450. However, after the closure of the hat factory around 1870 a decline set in to such an extent that the local rector was to write dejectedly in 1901 of some old families who once 'owned the soil' having become 'almost paupers upon it'. He complained of disappearing gentry, non-resident landowners and of men and boys eager to escape the village as soon as they could. By the time of the First World War just over half the local houses were either derelict or in need of extensive repairs.

In the 1920s and '30s urgently needed council houses appeared but it was from the '50s that better-off residents started to arrive eventually turning the virtually self-sufficient community of the past into a commuter one, deriving its inhabitants' incomes, many of their consumable goods and most of their more select entertainments from districts outside the area.

A list of relevant bibliographical references is available from Jeffery Spittal (01454 773158)

COALPIT HEATH

Lying, as it does, on a principal highway from Bristol, Coalpit Heath has attracted more notice in print from passing travellers and visitors than Frampton Cotterell. Here are four observations, two of them kindly and benevolent from journalists and two from scathing clerics:

From George Whitefield's journal on 30 March 1739:
'The place where I preached being near the maypole I took occasion to warn them of misspending their time in revelling and dancing. Oh, that all such entertainment were put a stop to.'

From F.E. Witts diary, rector of Upper Slaughter, Glos, on 8 April 1833:
'One tract of common over which we passed is called Coalpitheath, a ragged-looking spot, people and their dwellings being all out at the elbow. As we drew near to Bristol the country improved...'

From an article by J. Leech newspaper proprietor and journalist, from The Churchgoer [2nd Series, Bristol Rider, 1850] in 1844:
'Their [the local colliers] repugnance to use the newly consecrated churchyard and the habit which they have of leaving work immediately after an accident has occurred in any of the pits, [a] proneness to superstition [which] however has its counter advantages in the utter absence of infidelity, as well as in their great readiness to avail themselves of religious opportunities ...
There is too about the inhabitants and their dwellings a character of antiquity, a sort of simple and rude ancestral prestige [sic] attached to the place, which has an interest for those who look upon such things as indicative of more than outward appearance. Some of the farm houses seemed to be centuries old, with ceilings, carvings &c of the date of Elizabeth and James I ...
the people being generally in good condition, there being no actual poverty gives an air at once primitive and comfortable to the place and people'

From an article by W.J. Robinson, journalist and historian of West Country churches in the Bristol Times and Mirror, *17 June 1916:*

'If the intending visitor to Coalpit Heath imagines he is to be transported into an old-time village he will be disappointed. Very few villages however can boast of the large numbers of plum orchards to be seen there, which in early spring present a most charming picture of snowy whiteness. The trees give the scenery quite a character and distinction and the inhabitants for years have sustained a reputation for plum-growing. The only opportunity offered to antiquarians is a private house or two and three ancient hostelries. To those who love to entangle themselves among the cobwebs of past ages and whose hearts are turned towards stones, there may appear little in Coalpit Heath to attract them thither, but to those whose inclinations lead them to softer things and to the gentler scenes of nature, there are shady lanes, green meadows, picturesque nooks and many objects of rural interest. The houses are neat, and many have their fronts covered with a mantle of ivy, while quite a number stand in well-kept gardens which during the summer are gay with the brightest of flowers. Taking it all in all, Coalpit Heath, is a pleasant little place possessing an air of unceremonious prosperity and rural tranquillity.'

WINTERBOURNE

The village derives its name from the Bradley Brook and indicates that at one time its flow was limited to the winter period. Excavations at the Camp near Bury Hill suggest that there was a settlement here around 800BC and discovered artefacts which confirm occupation of the area by Iberians, Celts and Romans.

Court Farm next to the now isolated village church perhaps retains some part of the walls of the old manor house on the Bradestone family associated with Winterbourne during the fourteenth century at which time there was a gradual re-location of the village to its present hill-top plateau situation. Old farm houses such as Harcombe Farm and Hicks Farm in the Hicks Common Road area in the eastern part of the village would have had control of all that ground now covered by modern housing.

Minor names such as Flaxpits Lane and Tobacco Field suggest Tudor and Stuart cultivation. Wheat and barley also became important crops and John Aubrey observed in 1680 that turnips brought to Bristol eighty years previously entirely from Wales then came from the area of 'the red sand around Bristoll which they have found doth breed a better and bigger turnip'. In the nineteenth century market gardening developed producing tomatoes and the beds of stawberries available on a 'pick your own' plan until recent times.

Beneath the fertile marls which sustained such farming lies thePennant stone and where this is exposed and workable along the banks of the River Frome quarrying developed some 200 years ago, an industry in which theTillet family was prominent. The stone was used not only locally but also for some private and public buildings in the more prestigious suburbs of Bristol.

Winterbourne, like Frampton Cotterell, was involved in the hatting industry. Christies of Bermondsey established works in the village and also a family by the name of Vaughan both in the Watley's End area. Premises first used by hatters then became workplaces for the ready-made garment industry. The workforce was augmented by female 'outworkers' engaged in their tasks seven days a week. In 1907 in the Bristol area such workers were paid 5 to 8½d for trouser making, 4 to 8d for coats (which retailed at 8s) and 6 to 8d for vests. Thread had to be provided by the worker and a sewing machine either hired or paid for by instalments.

The concluding section of this book illustrates the building of the Wootton Bassett to Patchway main railway line through Winterbourne between 1897 and 1903. It was opened for goods traffic on 1 May 1903 and for passengers two months later. The section covering Winterbourne was a particularly difficult undertaking with its major viaduct, unstable ground and necessary embankments and cuttings. It is regrettable that no photograph has come to light of the workers' mission hut which was sited near Winterbourne Station.

One

Events

The committee in charge of organizing the Frampton Cotterell festivities to celebrate the Coronation of Edward VII in 1902. The gentleman in the centre (fifth from the left, second row from the back with the official badge and buttonhole is Dr R. Eager, superintendent of Northwoods House. Mr Harding, the meteorologist is in the high collar third from right in the back row.

The coronation celebrations of 1902 taking place in Frampton Cotterell. The pictures were taken at the western end of Church Road opposite the present Western Coach House pub. The old poor house building of 1824 can be seen in the left background in both pictures.

More celebrations in Church Road.

SKIPPING RACE CORONATION FRAMPTON COTTERELL

Some children take part in a skipping race in 1911.

More Coronation celebrations in Frampton Cotterell – this time in 1911 when George V came to the throne. The initials 'GR' can be seen on the cross-piece of the structure spanning the road. These pictures were taken outside Skinner's Yard. The Hambrook Brass Band provided the music.

A fancy dress parade with decorated bicycles line the road in front of the Cross Hands (now Western Coach House), Frampton Cotterell, *c.* 1920. The man in front of what may be the Hambrook Silver Band is a dignitary of some sort, perhaps connected with the church or parish council. The village policeman is keeping a watchful eye on proceedings from the back of the crowd.

An old age pensioners' outing from Coalpit Heath, September 1951. The Horse Shoe Inn lies to the left of the row of dwellings on the left of the picture. The Fire Engine Inn proclaims its identity from the roof and the gable end of Kate Davies' 'Hillside Stores' appears between the two. Kate Davies, who organized the trip, can be seen second from the right on the froun row.

A forced landing of a RAF de Havilland 'Gipsy Moth' biplane on ground now covered by Beesmoor Road, Coalpit Heath, on 17 August 1929.

The dedication of the War Memorial in the churchyard in Coalpit Heath, 1946.

The 1921 May Queen, Miss Ida Cox of Winterbourne Down. Behind can be seen Winterbourne Mill.

Winterbourne Down Womens' Institute visit the Houses of Parliament in the late 1940s. Left to right, back row: Gertie Withers, Ethel Bracey, Mary 'Maby' Walker, -?-, Peggy Vile, -?-, Patience Bethell, Mabel Vile, Jean Clark (from the post office), Mrs Harding. Second row from the back: Vera Davis, Agnes Britton, -?- (Mrs Hale's sister), Mrs Hale, Nora Mosley, Peggy Luff, Ian ?, Ida Cox, Mabel Smart, -?-, -?-, Laura Ludwell (Winterbourne PO), Elsie Prosser. Front row: -?-, Julie Thornell, -?-, Margery Jones, Arthur (?) Jones (Margery's son), Jennifer Jones (Margery's daughter), J.H. 'Bert' Alpass MP, Marg Coles, Kendal (?) Coles (Marg's son), Annice Collis, Marlene Thornell, Flo Walker, Mrs Palmer (the schoolmaster's wife), Mrs Eley, -?-.

Mrs Audrey Marks in Victorian costume chatting to Radio Bristol presenter 'Captain Courage' who opened the carnival held every May Day in Winterbourne Down.

Every Boxing Day the mummers and the ladies' Morris dance team can be seen performing outside the Cross Hands Inn, Winterbourne Down, at noon.

Two
Places and People

An early seventeenth-century house, No. 20 Frampton End Road, one of the few local residences of its type still surviving today. Members of the Bryant family pose for the camera.

BRISTOL ROAD

An early view of the Cross Hands, Bristol Road, taken around 1900. This hostelry lies practically at the geographical centre of Frampton Cotterell. Its present name, the Western Coach House, derives from the mistaken view that the building once offered hospitality to stage coach travellers *en route* to Gloucester. The coaching road, however, lay to the west, passing through Gaunt's Earthcott where a converted toll-house can still be seen. Older residents, some twenty years ago, spoke of the grounds of the pub being the site of bare-knuckle fights between local youths early in the nineteenth century.

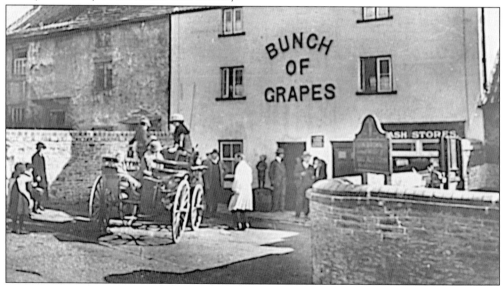

The Bunch of Grapes stood in Woodend Road and was later the premises used by Messrs Draisey, travelling hardware suppliers. Here the pub is the gathering point for an outing. The landlord's name is inscribed on a board on the wall by the door. The photograph was probably taken around 1920 and apart from the pub itself it is interesting to note the wretched external appearance of the cottage next door. This is a reminder of the fact that at the end of the First World War there were 340 houses in the village in need of repair (144 of them urgently), 37 unfit for habitation and a similar number overcrowded. In all 53.5% of the village housing was below standard – another possible reason for the flourishing pub trade!

Local carrier Mr Albert Tilling with his wife and children, *c.* 1910. The Tilling family lived in a cottage near the Swan at Nibley where Albert found local employment as a general carrier.

Riverside idyll: this locally published picture exemplifies a genre derived from Victorian popular illustrations. It was produced in 1922 by local corn and provision merchants, Rossiter and Rex.

For a couple of days at Christmas 1965 Frampton Cotterell was cut in two due to the overflowing of the River Frome. A new bridge was erected shortly afterwards.

In this shot of cottages opposite Skinner's Yard, Park Lane, Frampton Cotterell, the low chimney possibly indicated the presence of a domestic bakehouse. The one in the far distance is that of the waterworks. The rank of houses in the middle distance mark the end of Clyde Road and has now been replaced by modern bungalows.

Godfrey Elton, member of a well-known West Country family and a Fellow of Balliol College, Oxford, fought the Thornbury Constituency for Labour in the General Elections of both October 1924 and 1929, more than doubling his vote in that time. In 1929 he finished less than 500 votes behind the victorious Conservative and less than 200 behind the Liberal candidate, a result experts considered one of the most remarkable shifts of voting behaviour in the whole campaign. Elton remained in touch with the area until 1931 when, after the financial crisis of that year, he left Labour in sympathy with the views of his close friend, Ramsay MacDonald. To Party activists this was always remembered as an act of betrayal though many less politically committed felt a sense of almost personal loss. In 1938 Elton published *Among Others* an autobiographical work which includes a vivid and lively account of his local electioneering. He is pictured here with his dog 'Lossie' so called, perhaps, after Lossiemouth, MacDonald's Scottish birthplace.

On the private premises of the Community Association in School Road can be seen this wall plaque illustrating features of Frampton Cotterell's history. Composed of fifty-six tiles, it was the work of the Leyhill Resettlement Group from 1975 to 1976 of which the leading member and designer of the plaque was the former Newcastle City Councillor, T. Dan Smith.

Arthur Percival Rossiter (1903-1957). Son of a local corn and provision merchant, he received his first education at what is now Brockeridge School before proceeding to Bristol Grammar School in 1914. In 1924 he went to Selwyn College, Cambridge, where he took the first part of the Natural Sciences Tripos before switching to English in which he gained a First Class Degree in 1928. Teaching took him first to Japan and then to Durham University before he was admitted to a Fellowship in Jesus College, Cambridge, in 1945 and appointed to a tutorship in 1948. His principal interests were in drama up to the Elizabethans and in Shakespeare. He edited the anonymous play *Woodstock* dealing with the times of Richard II. He was, for a while, connected with the Basic English movement (which was involved in developing a simpler form of English to be used as an international language) and it was in Basic that he wrote a history of science. Apart from such wide-ranging scholarship, Rossiter was also an accomplished rower and fell climber. Following his death in 1957 at the age of fifty-three in an accident, a plaque was erected to his memory at Wasdale Head in Cumbria.

Mr Ernest Tovey in front of his cottage at the western end of Church Road, Frampton Cotterell. He is mounted on an interesting-looking vehicle.

A view of Step House (built 1733), formerly St Michael's Orphanage, in Park Lane, Frampton Cotterell. An interest in engaging women in useful social work arose in England during the 1850s stimulated by examples of such endeavours abroad, by the previous campaigning of Elizabeth Fry (1780-1845) and by the work of Florence Nightingale (1820-1910) in the Crimea. The title 'Sisters of Charity', adopted by those who managed St Michael's, was given currency in England by Mrs Anna Jameson (1794-1860) authouress of a comprehensive review of the problem which amounted to both a historical account and a social manifesto. Both the training of nurses and assistance given to the needs of poor children were components of the crusade. The community of St Michael's came to Frampton Cotterell in 1887 from the Herefordshire village of Garway and brought with them the name of the saint to whom Garway parish church is dedicated. The training of nurses predominated at this establishment, but in Frampton Cotterell orphanage work took over under the superintendency of Emily Dufaur Clark (1844-1927) who herself adopted one of the boys in the home.

Another view of Step House. There was accommodation for about three dozen juveniles including destitute children and orphans from various parts of the country. Boys stayed until they were fourteen and girls left at sixteen. Uniforms were provided for all when they left. An industrial department catered for girls over twelve who sought to be admitted to domestic service. The home closed shortly after 1919.

This is believed to be 'Sister' Clark.

Alonzo George Rowe who, when he left St Michael's Orphanage, went to work in Fry's chocolate factory in Bristol.

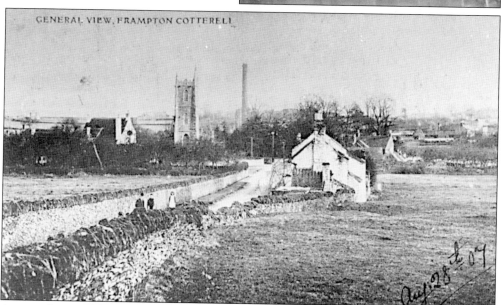

A general view of Frampton Cotterell looking east along Church Road in 1907. Apart from the Globe Inn and the church, all the other buildings have new disappeared. The field on the right was destined to become part of the Court Farm estate during the 1960s. The buildings belonging to the waterworks, including the distinctive tall chimney of the pumping house, may be seen in the group of trees in the centre of the photograph.

Rose Cottage, Harris Barton, Frampton Cotterell, *c.* 1908. Pictured is Mrs Eliza Brown and her son Alex (1903-1998) and daughter, Elsie.

Mrs Maud Long (left, with spectacles) who kept the general stores opposite Salem chapel, Winterbourne, between about 1920 and 1952. Her nephew, Mr Cyril Eackett, is on the extreme right standing behind his daughter, Monica. The photograph was taken in 1946.

The welcome home from the trenches of the First World War. Albert Taylor of Woodend Road, Frampton Cotterell, sits beside his father in a horse-drawn carriage.

The opening of Beesmoor Road, Frampton Cotterell, in 1928. The instigator of the building scheme was the Revd E.J. Phillips, vicar of St Saviour's from 1906 to 1936. Its construction provided the Woodend area of the village with a direct link to the Coalpit Heath main road. Prior to this the only access was an ascent by the hill leading to Zion chapel and so along Woodend Road as it exists today. The vicar also saw this enterprise as providing work for the unemployed and as a means of giving Frampton residents easier access to Coalpit Heath station. The name 'Beesmoor' appears as 'Bursemour' as early as 1301 and probably contains the Middle English surname 'Bursi' the meaning, therefore, being 'Bursi's moor'.

Beesmoor Road opening

Abstract from the June 1924 Church Magazine.

Some few months ago I (Rev E.J.Phillips) ventured to bring a matter of general interest before a parish meeting and was afterwards kindly invited to speak about it at a Parish Council meeting. I mean the question of making a new road to connect up the main road at Coalpit Heath with Beesmore and the Woodend part of Frampton Cotterell. There seems a good hope that the work will be carried out by the District Council in the near future. I feel sure that almost everyone will agree that it will be a convenience to the two parishes and incidentally provide work for some of the unemployed. It will save many a weary horse the steep pull up Brockridge Hill, and many a tired miner a rough ride and the bother of a turnstile at the end of Beesmore Lane. It will mean a direct route for Frampton people to the Station, and will be of great service in case of funerals from that part of our parish. The remark has been made that it may benefit some more than others. That usually happens with any public work, but it will hurt no one, and a broad minded person will naturally think of the benefit to the community. I think we shall all find our share of the benefit in one way or another. Those who live nearest may find the most.

The below photograph (shown by courtesy of Mrs Holbrook) is purported to be taken at the time of the Road opening in 1928. Canon Rev Phillips being shown in the centre.

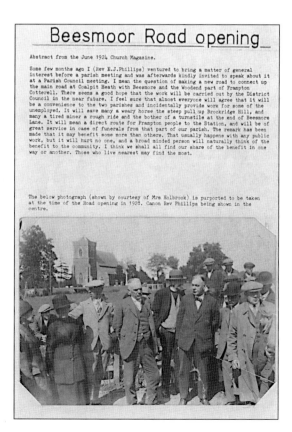

27

The Frampton Cotterell former poor house which was erected in 1824 at a time when villages throughout England were responsible for the destitute of their parish. The crude beginnings of photography were still twelve years in the future but the building survived to be clearly visible in the pictures of the 1902 coronation celebrations shown on p. 10. The tender approved by the Vestry amounted to £179 for which the occupants were allocated approximately 80sqft of accommodation surrounded by thick walls together with heat from a fireplace with flues in the party wall. The building covered the ground at the rear of what is now 413-419 Church Road which incorporated yet another village pub – the Stagg's (sic) Head – which continued to trade until the outbreak of the First World War. Now only the horse trough remains.

The Millpond, Frampton Cotterell.

A postcard sent from Frampton Cotterell in 1905. On the back Carrie apologises to Miss Bailey for forgetting the 9th August'.

Another postcard sent from Frampton Cotterell, this time in 1908. This one is addressed to Miss Hill in Redland and expresses concern for 'E.B.' for whom 'Florence fetched Dr J. this morning' but the recipient is advised 'Don't worry, dear. It may pass off again if she keeps warm'.

Mr C. Bowyer of Frampton Cotterell in fancy dress as Buffalo Bill.

William Tovey and a friend in Alexandra Road, Frampton Cotterell, with a couple of magnificent bicycles.

Mr Henry Herbert Harding (1870-1951) came to Frampton Cotterell from Fishponds in 1905 when he purchased Park House in Park Row. Here he ran a market garden business. Meteorology was his great hobby and in Frampton Cotterell he carried on the series of recordings he had begun in Fishponds in 1883 and continued up until his death. By 1895 his work had already earned him a Fellowship of the Royal Meteorological Society and from 1896 he began contributing weather notes to the local press. He provided forecasts for the *Bristol Evening News* until it ceased publication. He was also involved in compiling annual reports for the Bristol Medical Officer of Health and in work for the Meteorological Office which, in the 1930s, designated Park House as a climatological station. For five years after H.H. Harding's death the records were maintained by his son, Mr Alec Harding and so constitute an invaluable fifty-year chronology of local weather observations.

Henry Herbert Harding's notes for January 1883.

A house stood on the Northwoods estate in the outer boundaries of Frampton Cotterell at least as far back as the 1770s but the building we see today was erected after Henry Hawes Fox (1769-1852) had purchased the estate in 1832. It was intended for the provision of 'an extensive Asylum for the Insane' into which he incorporated a pioneer system of fireproof flooring which was patented in 1844 and not superseded for domestic use until 1873. When erected around a quarter of the available places at Northwoods was reserved for the poor of the parish – at a time when settlement in the village poorhouse was due to be replaced by the less congenial provisions of the Chipping Sodbury Workhouse. For a year after the death of H.H. Fox his son William Charles Fox managed the asylum before taking Holy Orders and becoming rector of Frampton Cotterell in 1872. The last Medical Superintendent retired in 1956.

Northwoods laundry maids pictured around 1920.

NORTHWOODS ——— Winterbourne, Bristol.

This beautiful mansion in fifty acres of delightful grounds was built specially for the treatment of NERVOUS AND MENTAL AILMENTS, ALCOHOLISM AND DRUG ADDICTION.

Voluntary, temporary or certified patients of both sexes.

A few voluntary patients are also received in the Medical Superintendent's House.

Separate bedrooms. Private suites. Central heating. Electric light. Ample facilities for amusements and employment. Private golf course.

Thorough clinical, bacteriological and pathological examinations.

Occupational therapy. Visiting consultants. Garden and dairy produce from farm on the estate.

Cars meet trains at Temple Meads and Stapleton Road Stations. A private car or ambulance sent any distance day or night for patients.

Terms from 4 guineas a week.

Medical Superintendent—
JOSEPH CATES, M.D., B.S. (Lond.), D.P.H. (Camb).

Telephone & Telegraph—
WINTERBOURNE 18.

An advertisement for Northwoods dating from 1903. The same problems seemed to exist then as today.

Park Lane, Nos 134-136. These are good examples of the older houses in the village possibly first erected as one 'long-house' with accommodation for both humans and their animals. Much of what can be seen today belongs to the seventeenth century although during the eighteenth the property was re-roofed and the eaves raised to give more room in the attics. The division of the house took place at the same time and the porch is an irrelevant addition of later date. Note the difference in the forms of stonework, the blocked-in windows and the dripstones (an early form of guttering) above them.

Day House', 56 School Road. In a glossary of Gloucestershire dialect published in 1890 the word is quoted as 'dey-house' (pronounced dey'us) and explained as meaning a dairy or 'house where cheese is made'. The situation of the property on the limits of the former extent of Frampton Court suggests the existence of such a building serving the needs of the inhabitants of the Court.

The Homestead, Badminton Road, built in 1931 by a brother of Samuel Stone, one-time licensee of the Half Moon Inn. The brother had spent some time in the United States and the name of the 'American House' accorded to it by local residents was quite appropriate in view of the railed one storey extension, a very New England building style. It was demolished in the 1960s to make room for a car sales display area.

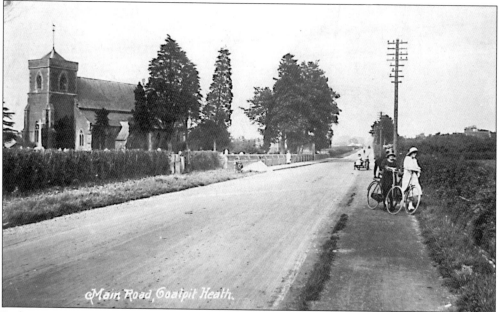

Badminton Road, Coalpit Heath, c. 1920. As can be seen, there was plenty of room for both motorists and pedestrians in the middle of the highway and no housing development on the left hand side of the road beyond the church. The two girls in the picture are Lily Smart and her sister.

34

A view of the Half Moon Inn, Coalpit Heath, possibly around 1900. The pub was demolished in the early 1960s and a replacement built which itself has now been demolished and replaced by a totally new 'Badminton Arms'.

Mr Fred Stone outside Mafeking Hall, opened in 1946. Now South Cotswold District Scout HQ, Serridge Lane, Coalpit Heath.

Originally known as Bitterwell Pond this stretch of water was bought from the colliery by Mr C. Newman in 1930 and presented to Westerleigh Parish Council.

Norman Crew (left) and Fred Stone (right) at Bitterwell Lake which was created originally to form a reservoir of water for colliery engines serving pits sunk in the area during the early days of mining development.

A property in Bristol Road, Frampton Cotterell, pictured in the early years of the twentieth century. It would appear to have stables adjoining.

Mr and Mrs Gowen and their son who lived in 'The Gully' off Factory Road, Watley's End.

A Watley's End family, identity unknown.

All activity in Watley's End is suspended as a couple out in a pony and trap and pedestrians give their attention to the photographer. This is thought to be Rectory Road.

Born in 17 March 1880, the son of Daniel and Jane Matthews (née Grindle) at 'The Grove', High Street, Winterbourne, Harry Grindell Matthews became one of the most fertile (and most commonly forgotten) inventors of the last century. He began his work by designing a light-controlled boat to be used as an anti-submarine weapon and in the detonation of mines and then turned to a 'sky projector' and a 'Lunatone' which used broken rays of light as a means of composing music. As war approached in 1939 he worked on the idea of an 'Aerial Minefield', a torpedo fired from the ground carrying a cluster of rockets to be exploded by a time fuse. It was his development of an invisible ray capable of destroying solid objects which earned him his name of 'the death-ray man'. There were also experiments on the talking films conducted in 1921 at the New Passage Hotel at Pilning. His chronic lack of any business acumen allowed that work to be appropriated by the Americans. Courted by officialdom but never given practical assistance for his inventions Matthews retired in 1934 to 'The Cloud', a lonely bungalow fitted out as an experimental laboratory, at Mynyddygwais near Swansea. It was there that he died in 11 September 1941.

This house on the left is 'The Grove' in Winterbourne. It was the home of the Matthews family into which H.G. Matthews was born in 1880.

Victoria Lodge, Nicholls Lane, Winterbourne, which was owned in the 1930s by Mr and Mrs Harrison who rented rooms to young married couples. This property has now given way to modern flats called Nicholls Court.

Swan Lane, Winterbourne, with children playing on the Green. On the left stood a shop which disappeared in the 1950s. It had been run since 1933 by the Buckley family who had a daughter called Audrey. On the right can be seen the entrance to Crossley Farm.

Cottages built on Bacon, or Beacon, Lane, Winterbourne, around 1840. This photograph was taken around 1900. The first dwelling was home to the Shiptons, the second to Joe Parker and the third was occupied by a family called Alden. The fourth building housed a pub, the Lion Inn, which brewed its own beers. Boilers can still be seen in the walls. The first tenant, in 1840, was Mrs Louisa Tucker. In 1880 William Fowler sold out to Hall and Gibbs brewery. Another tenant was Bagsy Andrews and around 1935/36 Mr and Mrs Lyons took over. The family still live in the house, the only building in the row to survive.

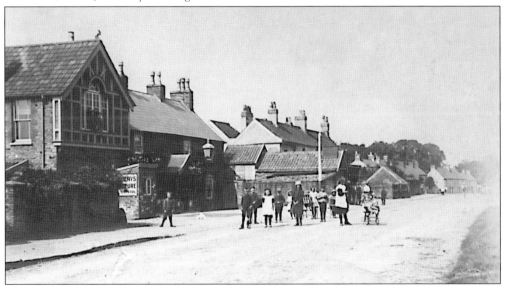

A wealth of historical detail is found in this photograph of High Street, Winterbourne, from the turn-of-the-century clothes worn by the children to the weighbridge office – the small building in front of the pub. A steel plate can be seen in front. This feature was present in most villages to enable the farmers to weigh their lorries before going to market to sell their goods. Where the group of men stand was a General Stores. The rank of cottages in the distance is Donkey Terrace.

Donkey Terrace, Winterbourne, – so called because a man called Charlie Jones lived in the end house and kept a donkey in the adjoining field. It was also known as Rotten Row because it was once the village Poorhouse.

Tom Walker, from Winterbourne, who served in the army during the First World War as a hairdresser in Egypt. When he was demobbed his parents had died and his family's attitude was unwelcoming so he took to the road. He was a friendly man who visited a niece in Hambrook for a bath and a change of clothes. He always wore a buttonhole of wild flowers and more blooms in his cap. He was a religious man and when the village children asked him for the text for the day he would quote them a verse from the Bible.

Resting by the river: Tom Walker died on 31 January 1961 and is buried at Winterbourne Church.

The fishpond in Winterbourne. Barton Cottage with its thatched roof is on the left.

Barton Cottage, Winterbourne, when it had had its roof tiled and new gables built.

The gable of Barton cottage, bearing the date when it was built.

Thomas Marks walking up Church Lane, Winterbourne, *c.* 1910.

This picture was taken in Winterbourne Down by a local photographer called Hepworth around 1922 and the people at the end of the road can be identified. The boy with the bike is Bill Noad and the girl, Miss Curry, who lives at the top of Harcombe Hill. In the horse-drawn cart can be seen Tom and Gus Luton from Ivory Hill.

An up-to-date photograph taken from the same spot. Three new bungalows have appeared – two on the lower slope of the hill, the third replacing the old village hall.

Winterbourne Mill in the background together with the outbuildings and owner's cottage. The shop was run by William Jones (brother of Robert) who carried out boot and shoe repairs and also sold sweets. One of the signs outside the store states 'Good Boating'. It would have been possible to row upstream all the way to Frampton Cotterell. The picture was taken in the late 1890s.

The bottom of Mill Steps, close up of the owner's cottage.

The Weir, Winterbourne Mill.

Three sisters – Agnes, Annie and Elsie Cordy – pictured outside their house in Church Road, Winterbourne Down, in the early 1900s.

The Cordy family had a market garden on the right hand side of Harcombe Hill. Pictured harvesting flowers is Agnes who by now had married and was called Britton.

Harcombe Farm, Winterbourne, a sixteenth-century building, home to the Pendock family from about 1788 until 1953 when it was taken over by the Cryers. The Pendock family are seen here around 1890. Left to right: Auntie Mary, Harold Wallington (her nephew), Martha, Henry (with the pitchfork, who took over the farm from his father), Mary and Alfred Wallington (seated). Mary died in 1904 aged eight-seven. Next to Alfred is Sarah Ellen (wearing a hat), Harriet, Thomas Bridgeman Pendock (with bike). Thomas died in 1894 aged seventy-seven years. Behind him are Emma Wallington and an unknown boy with a donkey.

The Pendock family in the 1930s. There were six sisters and four brothers. In this group second from left is Henry, fourth is Martha and sixth is Celia standing next to Harold Wallington.

Cross Roads, Winterbourne Down.

Taken in the early 1920s this picture shows Mrs Maynard, landlady of the Cross Hands Inn with a young companion.

The same scene in the 1960s by which time a bungalow had been built on the left and a wooden air force hut (left) dating from the First World War had been brought from Filton to become the home of Mrs Evans.

Three
Religion

The Wesleyan chapel, Frampton Cotterell. The Country Stores, seen to the left, closed in May 2000. The site of the chapel is now No. 153 Church Road. Built in 1821 as a direct result of a strongly evangelical campaign conducted locally from 1818 by a breakaway group of Wesleyan Methodists. They used large tents erected in the Frampton End and Mays Hill districts and an outlying barn on the site of a modern house nearer Iron Acton still carrying that name. The chapel passed into official Methodist custody in 1932.

A Sunday School treat at the Wesleyan Methodist chapel, Church Road, Frampton Cotterell, 1906.

A similar occasion taking place at the chapel in 1932. This was declared the Centenary Year, dating from the registration of the building as Methodist Church property after the demise of the 'Tent Methodists'. The hut situated behind the church was ex-Army property removed from Salisbury Plain at the end of the First World War.

The Revd J. Claude Hearle, Wesleyan Methodist minister at Frampton Cotterell from 1919 to 1925 and again from 1936 to 1940, pictured here with his wife, Elsie.

The congregation of Bethel chapel enjoying a treat in the early part of the twentieth century. In 1851 Frampton Cotterell acquired its second Methodist chapel. Known as 'Bethel' it was situated in Woodend Road near the present post office and it belonged to the United Free Methodists, a substantial breakaway movement from the Wesleyan body which lost sixteen of its local pew-holders to its new rival. Gradually throughout the rest of the century Wesleyan membership totals recovered from its mid-century schisms. The chapels, along with the pubs, were then the social foci of the village and, for the children, the only one. Local schools did not cater for extracurricular activities as they do today. The last Methodist chapel in the village was built on The Ridge for the Primitive Methodists in 1887 with ten of its thirteen trustees being miners (ten out of fifteen in 1904). Reunited in 1932 as the 'Methodist Church' the three chapels kept going until 1967 by the end of which year they were all closed and most of their former congregations were preparing for a new era of joint worship at Zion chapel.

53

More Bethel chapel worshippers arrayed in their best clothes in the same era.

Late Mr JOHN TANNER GREEN,
who was Sunday School Superintendent
at Bethel, Frampton Cotterell,
for nearly 40 years.

Called Home, Sunday, November 15th, 1914.
Aged 77 years.

Mr John Tanner Green (1837-1914) superintendent of the Bethel Sunday School for nearly forty years.

The interior of Zion chapel. The magnificent organ was installed in 1910 resulting from the generosity of a benefactor. By 1820 the Sunday School had 200 children on the roll and from here similar classes were developed in neighbouring villages. Until 1844 the Sunday preachers supplied by the Bristol Congregational Itinerant Society walked the nine miles in and out of the city. There were only two 'permanent appointments' to the pulpit, both short-lived. The eighteen members of the original church steadily grew in number and in 1815 the building was 'altered and improved'. In 1834 new galleries were added. The ministry of the Revd W. Mends Howell from 1865 to 1873 was so successful that there was need for a new chapel. 'Zion' has always remained unaffected by divisions and successions with an apparently higher profile than the local Methodist groups. From 1968 it has been a joint Methodist/United Reformed church, only the third of such unions to be effected in this country.

Zion chapel outing, c. 1920. Mr Stan Thornell and his wife, Lillie, are at the back of the vehicle and Mr Ernest Tovey is standing at the front.

Frampton Cotterell Male Voice Choir which was associated with Zion chapel, 1926.

An interior view of St Peter's church. The church is austerely Tractarian with admonitory scrolls beneath the clerestory windows. One of the stained glass windows dating from 1882 commemorates Edward Bouverie Pusey (1800-1882). On the wall of the south aisle is a plaque to John Symes, MP for Somerset 1623/24, and his wife Amy who found refuge in the village during the Civil War period which would indicate local allegiance to the Royalist cause. There is also a parish chest with its mandatory furniture of three locks ensuring it could only be opened by the incumbent in the presence of two churchwardens.

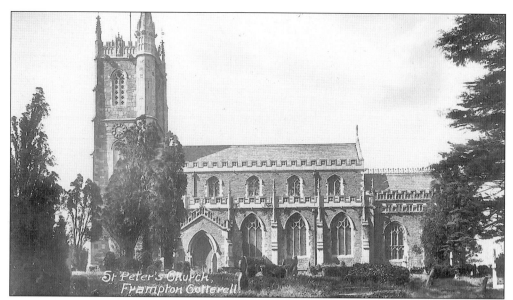

The exterior of the church. Part of the tower is all that remains of the medieval church erected on this site, the high altar of which was dedicated in 1315. The rest of the building is a Perpendicular style restoration of 1858 which incorporated a new north aisle and additions to the south side of the chancel. Some £10,000 of the necessary finance came from the Revd William Charles Fox, son of Henry Hawes Fox, first superintendent of Northwoods House Asylum, who was assistant curate in 1858 before becoming rector in 1872. The architect was John Norton (1823-1904), a busy church builder and restorer both in and around Bristol and in the valleys of South Wales – to say nothing of other commissions for work on Lundy Island, at Totland Bay and in Estonia!

The induction of the Revd Charles A. MacConochie in 1911. He is the tall figure in the centre of the middle row flanked by the Rt Revd G.F. Brown, Bishop of Bristol, on his left and Dr Burder, a cleric who lodged at the rectory for many years (and was rarely to be seen outside it) on his right. Next to Burder is Mr C. Smith who later came to take a leading role in village choral performances. The dark-suited man on the extreme right is Mr Drew, the church organist. The Revd MacConochie served as rector until 1943.

The Salvation Army food cart. The Salvation Army began its work in Frampton Cotterell in Clyde Road in 1882 and remained in the same premises until 1957. The food cart was a once-only event in September 1914 and the vehicle was hired from a Mr Anstey of Watley's End. It delivered food to the needy and on its journey collected suitable donations for subsequent redistribution.

St Saviour's church, Coalpit Heath. A new church for a new parish when, in April 1845, Coalpit Heath parish was constituted out of Nibley and parts of Westerleigh and Frampton Cotterell. It was built in 1844/45 by the distinguished architect William Butterfield (1814-1900) and with original provision for 500 sittings. It is in the style of fourteenth-century parish church design though generally regarded as a competent 'thesis' exercise devoid of any of those flamboyant stylistic idioms which came to characterize Butterfield's later and larger commissions. The architect also designed all the original internal fittings. In keeping with the whole historical concept is the striking lych-gate of solid geometrical composition.

St Saviour's vicarage. This is generally regarded by architectural historians as a landmark building. It was erected at the same time as the church and revived a Cotswold vernacular style though with modification of window design and the positioning of the massive chimney breasts. The significant claim to notice in the design is that the elevation rises directly out of the plan with the rooms not 'packed into a preconceived uniform shell'. One therefore does not have to guess at the disposition of the internal accommodation behind a standard, virtually unadorned, flat frontage. One writer has identified the vicarage as 'middle class in the best sense' and it was certainly for middle class well-to-do clients that later developments of the style were created most notably in the work of Richard Norman Shaw (1931-1912).

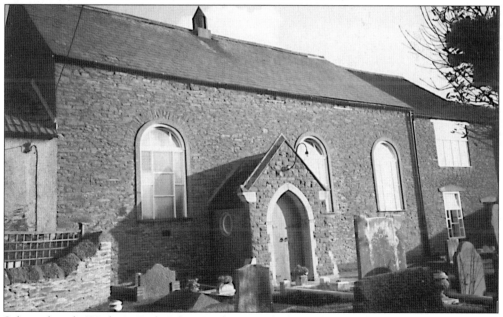

Salem chapel, Watley's End. John Wesley preached on the foundation of this chapel on 17 September 1787.

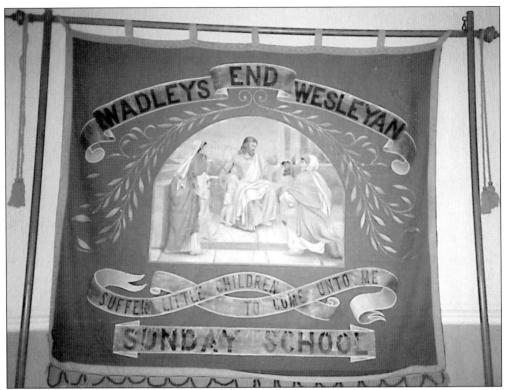

The Salem banner showing the old spelling of Watleys End – 'Wadley's End'

Ebenezer Primitive Methodist chapel, Watley's End, pictured in the 1890s. A growing demand for another Methodist chapel meant that land was purchased for £15 from the Vaughans and the building was opened to worshippers in 1868. The name means 'Hitherto the Lord has helped us'.

Winterbourne church. Parts of the building date back to pre-Norman times although it is mostly the work of fourteenth-century architects. The spire has twice been struck by lightning. It was last restored in 1951. The oldest monument in the church is that of Thomas de Bradstone, Governor of Gloucester and a great military and naval hero. In one of the cottages clustered round the church lived Alice and Thomas Marks, grandparents of one of the authors, Syd Marks. They lived in the house from 1896 to 1914 and their son James was born there.

Bell ringers. It is thought this photograph dates from the 1930s. Left to right, back row: Ernie Thomas, C. Curtis, Fred Smart, George Manning, Steve Shipway. Front row: Walt Cornish, Frank Curtis, Billy Barton.

The upper churchyard and the old rectory in Winterbourne Down built in 1860. In the centre is the church school which was built in 1866. The large dip in the foreground is now filled with trees.

An early photograph of All Saints church, Winterbourne Down, showing the bell tower on the right (rather than the left as seen on the following page) and without the steps to the lower churchyard (also see following page). The church was built in 1858 and was designed by George Edmund Street (1824-1881).

The bell tower was moved to the left in 1949. The steps were constructed in 1912. They were dedicated to the memory of the Revd William Henderson who died in 1910.

The vicarage as it was in 1867. It was built in 1860.

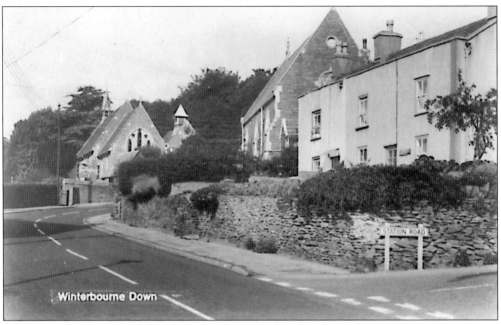

All Saints church on the left with Bethesda Methodist church on the right.

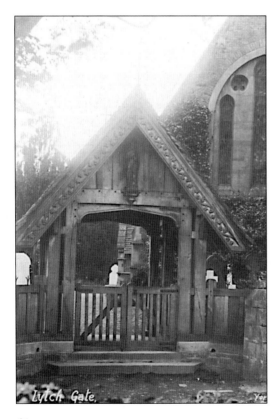

The lych-gate was built in 1914 in memory of F.W. Greenstreet who died on 17 April 1913, aged eighty-six.

A private memorial to two of the sons of a former churchwarden, the elder of whom was killed in the First World War. The family very kindly allowed the names of local men who had lost their lives in battle to be added to the plinth. After the Second World War the name of a grandson (D.G.G. Coles, a rugby international) was inscribed there, also those of his aircrew who died with him.

A photograph of the interior of the church taken by Hamiltons of Staple Hill in 1914.

All Saints church choir, 1946. They are led by Mr Harold Badman carrying the cross. The pairs of choristers are: Sydney Marks and Michael Woods, Keith Walters and Paul Huish, Clive Tovey, Michael Sterling and Richard Evans. The Revd John Nobbs brings up the rear.

Mr Frederick Greenstreet, the first incumbent.

The Revd Frederick Bishop with his family. He founded the Hambrook Band. He and his wife, Laura, had nine children.

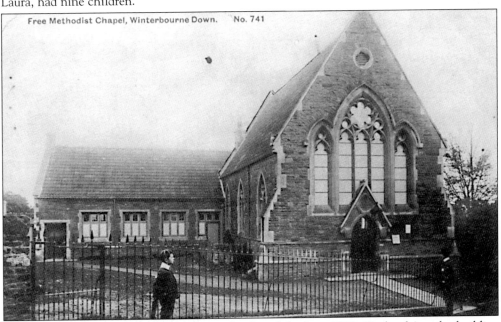

Free Methodist Chapel, Winterbourne Down.   No. 741

Winterbourne Down United Free Methodist chapel, built in 1879. 'Bethesda' as the building was subsequently known had its origins as an infant's school founded on land sold by a group of Bristol and Thornbury businessmen together with a grocer, two hatters and a shoemaker from Winterbourne in which an occasional Sunday School could be held as well as meetings 'of a religious and moral tendency'. In time the 'poor man's chapel' as it was known came to accommodate more of such meetings and, while the school faltered, demand for an appropriate place of worship grew to such an extent that better premises were demanded. It was agreed to build this entirely new place of worship on the site of the former school.

Some of the congregation pictured outside in the 1940s.

A chapel outing, again in the 1920s. From the back: -?-, Florrie Walker, John Walker, -?-, Mrs Walker, -?-, Stan Crew (at back), Mrs Crew, Mrs Vera Davis, Arthur Davis, ? Thomas, Jack Prosser, ? Prosser, -?-, Reg Maggs, -?- (at front), Charlie Britton, Mrs Britton, Annie Cordy, Doris Cox, ? Ricketts, Mr Evans, Bertha Evans, Annie Badman, Lillian Lloyd, -?-, -?-, -?-, -?-, ? Maggs, -?-, -?-, the driver, Frank Mann.

Four

Schools

Going to school in Frampton Cotterell before the First World War. Most of the girls wear pinafores to protect their dresses and the boys sport Eton collars and Norfolk jackets.

The former National School, in School Road, Frampton Cotterell, was erected 1854/56 on land given by George Bengough, Lord of the Manor, in 1842. From 1843 to 1846 schooling took place in two club rooms, part of the New Inn in Mill Lane, adjacent to St Peter's church. The first two classes consisted of eighty boys and eighty girls. By 1847 a purpose-built structure annexed to the church came into use. It was demolished ten years later when the church was rebuilt and the school was then brought into association with the National Society for the Education of the Poor in the Principles of the Established Church, so standing in contrast to the 'British School' in Woodend Road. The building was also used for meetings of the parish council until its closure in 1969. It is now called Crossbow House and has been the home of the local Community Association since 1975.

Henfield Road with Coalpit Heath Manor School on the left.

A new school was built in the High Street in Winterbourne in 1869 and it was called St Michael's.

A photograph of St Michael's dating from the 1890s showing a teacher in one of the lovely dresses of the period. The headmaster, Alfred Day, stands on the right. He held the post from 1885 to 1915 and was well-liked by the children. Mr Syd Marks who provided these photographs remembers his parents speaking highly of Mr Day.

Mr Day again with staff and pupils including one of the author's father, Mr James 'Jim' Marks' who is in the second row, third from left in 1904. He was born in 1898 and lived in one of the cottages near the church.

One solitary girl among a class of boys in the 1930s. Was she, perhaps, a pupil teacher? No traffic disturbs the group. In the background, on the right, is the Wheatsheaf.

Winterbourne School in 1935. Left to right, back row: Erine Anstey, Ron Bignell, Alec Hacker, Ken Bisp, Richmond Jones. Second row from the back: Ron Knapp, Mavis Anstey, Marion Cornish, Betty Rodman, Enid Maggs, Phylis Lewis, ? Berry. Third row: Roy Anstey, Hazel Anstey, Olive Thornel, Dolly Knapp, Maggie Manning, Marion Lloyd, Margaret Wickham, Ivor Player. Front row: Clift Lowe, Fred Cane, ? Berry, Gilbert Thyne, Dick Whithead, John Anstey.

Winterbourne Down Infants School, 1920. Some names are known. Left to right, sanding at the back: Alan Badman, Bill Flook, Mildred Cox, -?-, -?-, Joan Flook, -?-, ? Monks, Miss Lilian Rodgers (teacher from Hambrook). Second row frin the back, seated: Hubert Flook, -?-, -?-, Trevor Bird, -?-, -?-, Percy Cordy, -?-. Third row: -?-, Ivy Turner, -?-, Doris Cox, Mrs Smith (teacher), -?-, -?-, Kathleen Lockyer, Stanley Monks. Front row: -?-, -?-, Betty Pendock, -?-, Ron Pincott, -?-, Herbert Adams.

All Saints Church School, Winterbourne Down, was designed by Edward William Godwin (1833-1886), a progressive architect. It was opened in 1866 and enlarged in 1889 to mark the Jubilee of the church. In July 1944 it became a junior school (Under Elevens) and finally closed on 28 July 1961. It is now a privately owned house.

Another group of prettily dressed children from All Saints School with their teachers, c. 1920.

A class from the turn of the century. Teachers at the school over the years have been: Miss K. Smith (Head 1945-61), Mrs Lena Evans, Mrs Paddock, Mrs Streadwick, Miss Read, Miss Jones, Miss Hardy, Miss Balch, Mr Morris (Head), Mr Renshaw (Head 1940-42), Mr and Mrs Noyce (Head 1891-96) Miss Chitty, Mr Martin and Mrs Pagewood (both 1914-18).

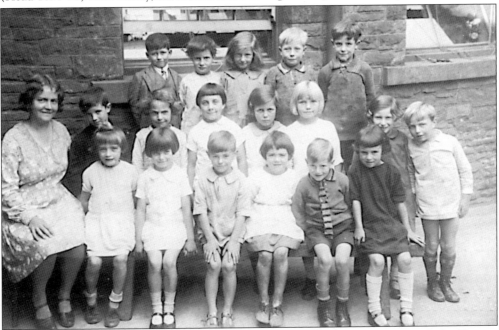

Winterbourne Down School, 1929/30. Left to right, back row: Dennis Tovey, Ruby Turner, Betty Waters, Windsor Monks, -?-. Middle row: Miss Jones, Max Evans, Edna Parsons, Joyce Flook, Gladys Close, Iris Evans, -?-, Eric Parsons. Front row: Rose Glastonbury, Cynthia Palmer, Tom Pendock, Jenny Adams, Norman Petrie, Eunice Lloyd.

The same school pictured on a summer's day. The teacher is Miss Hardy. Left to right, back row: Fred Skuse, Betty Waters, Joyce Flook, Norman Petrie. Second row from the back: ? Luton, Jesse Turner, George Newman, Stephanie Skuse, Jenny Adams, Windsor Monks, Dorothy Glastonbury. Front row: George Luton, Eric Parsons, Roy Morris, Desmond (or Donald) Tovey, Rose Glastonbury, Tom Pendock, Eunice Lloyd.

The school in, it is thought, 1926. Left to right, back row: William Glastonbury, Bill Stollard, Cecil Luton, Ralph Cook, Willie Young, Wink Stanley, Geoff Palmer. Second row from the back: Doug Reece, Frances Turner, Gladys Cordy, Marion Langdon, Winnie Lloyd, Irne Skuse, Hilda Andrews, Vivian Maggs, Joyce Florence, Miss Balch (who took classes 3 and 4). Third row: Dorothea Tuck, Ella Williams, Queenie Turner, Jessie Monks, Doris Evans, Betty Pendock, Marion Robertson. Front row: Fred Luton, Jimmy England, Stan Glastonbury, Richard Hurst, Doug Reece, Hedley Turner, George Lloyd.

Another generation pictured in 1949. Some of the children's names are unknown as they were from the Downend Homes for Orphans. To the left, back row, are: Mrs Thornell, Mrs Bethel and Margaret Evans. The woman in the dark dress on the right is dinner lady Monica Prendergast and next to her is Linda Goodfield. Pam Skuse is second from right in the front row. The two teachers in the centre are Mrs Evans and Miss Smith. Among the others present are: Roy Close, Tony Trueman, Alan Wheeler, Linda Manning, Mildred Clancey, Melba Rowlands, Veronica Ferris, Esme Pincott, Roger Hunter, Maureen Smith, Jean Evans, Ruth Lewis, Jennifer Jones (with the big bow in front of Miss Smith), Margaret Thomas, Janet Skuse, June Prendergast.

Last days at the school with Mrs Evans and Miss Smith surrounded by pupils.

Another group from the 1940s/50s. The dinner ladies are Mrs Manning and Mrs Bethel and the teachers Miss Smith and Mrs Evans.

May Day at the school with the girls dancing and the maypole at a rather precarious angle.

The boys lead this time. Miss Smith, the headmistress, regards the maypole with some concern. In the background can be spotted the vicar, Revd Nobbs.

Winterbourne Down School football team, winners of the trophy 1924/25. Left to right, back row: Len Stanley, Les Maggs, Albert Maggs, Jack Cordy. Middle row: Mr Morris (headmaster) Lionel Stallard, Maurice Counsell, Jeff Stanley. Front row: Eric Evans, George Thomas, Alan Badman, Doug Bird, Jack Lloyd.

The team during the 1922/23 season. Left to right, back row: Len Stanley, Maurice Counsell, P. Wheeler, Alan Badman, W. Turner, Len Pincott, R. Counsell, A. Turner. Middle row: E. Bryant, W. Skuse, F. Carey, Doug Bird, H. Thomas. Front row: H. Clark, R. Bird, L. England, Albert Luff.

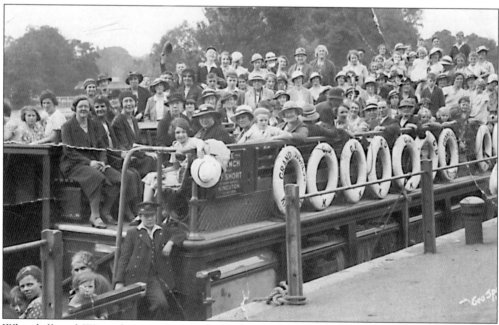

Whitehill and Winterbourne Down schools boat trip, 1935. Among the trippers are Gladys Maggs, Jessie Mathews, Annie Badman, Dorothy Ricketts, Mrs and Mrs Christopher Churchill, Maisie Fowler. The little girl in her mother's arms is Valerie Maggs.

Five
Sport and Leisure

Frampton Cotterell football team, 1936/37 season.

Billy Harbutt and his brother Leslie were members of the 1934 Frampton Cotterell football team. Chick Thornell is the mascot.

PAS DE LIEU RHÔNE QUE NOUS.

Everything is ready for the presentation of the cups at the end of the 1934 season.

Coalpit Heath Tennis Club, *c.* 1920. Left to right, back row: Louie Curtis, Doris Blackmore, Victoria Williams, -?-, Sylvester Tovey, -?-, -?-, Mrs Harding, Mr Harding, Cyril Bass, -?-, -?-. Middle row: Charlie Smith, Grace Barrington, -?-, -?-, Jack Barrington, Doris Curtis (?), Carrie Hopkins, Mrs Pullin, Percy Varlow. Front row: Gilbert Dando, Louie Vardon, Reg Dando.

The Coalpit Heath cricket team in 1901. Left to right, back row: J. Bryant, F. Tovey, J. Crew, S. Bateman, G. Smart (vice captain), C. Newman, Revd F.W. Griffiths (president). Middle row: E. Cook (honorary secretary), C. Tremlin, F. Cook (captain), G. Watson, H. Tremlin (then an Essex County professional but formerly a CPH player). Front row: F. Fowler. H. Alsop.

The opening of the cricket club pavilionat Coalpit Heath in 1910.

The Coalpit Heath cricket team, 1929.

Cricket has been played here from a time before the Manor School, Coalpit Heath, was opened in 1869. This picture shows the former full range of buildings with the head teacher's house closing the facade on the right.

Watley's End football team in 1918. Left to right, back row: Jim McCrae, -?-, Bill Buckley, Alex Smart, Bill Hacker, ? Gifford, -?-, Jim Maggs, -?-. Middle row: -?-, Charlie Britton, Harry Gifford. Front row: Albert Nicholls, -?-, -?-, Jack Eastman, George Tovey.

Winterbourne football team, 1926/27. Among those pictured here are: Gaily Maggs, Sonny Sargent, Vic Thompson, Herbert Lyons, Harold Badman, Jack Eastman, Edwin Bishop, Raymond Dandop, Gilbert Allsop, Joe Scott.

The football team in the 1933/34 season.

The 1949/50 team. Left to right, back row: L. Kislingbury, John Bennett, John Lloyd, Eric Allsop, Harold England, Dennis Timbrell George Newman, Maurice Hacker,Cliff Phipps. Front row: Richard Evans, Brian Mathews, Brian Kislingbury, Martin Rutter, David Haskins.

Winterbourne Down football team, 1908/09, pictured outside the Star Inn at Pye Corner. This was a postcard sent by Graham Evans to George Cordy with the bad news that he had lost his job at Huckford Quarry. The man on the far right wearing a cap is Billy Alden: in the middle row the first on the left is Mr Manning and Graham Evans himself is in the middle of the front row.

The Winterbourne Down Women's Institute. Left to right, back row: May Anstey, Net Newman, Elsie Prosser, Agnes Britton (sister to Elsie), Ida Cox (their niece), Mrs Hale, Miss Butcher, Evelyn Newman, Vera Davis (née Tuck), Doris Rutter, Patience Bethell, May Harrison, Blanche Vile, Mrs Brookman (the baker's wife), Marg Coles. Middle row: Mrs Mapstone, Gertie Withers (Jack's wife), Mabel Vile, Mrs Roberts, Alice Crosman, Phylis Kislingbury, Alice Tuck, Flo Walker. Front row: Lizzy Maggs, Ethel Bracey, Nora Mosley, Freda Turner, Dawn Kislingbury.

Winterbourne Brownies from the 1940s. Left to right, back row: -?-, Christine Morgan, Joyce Bethell, Betty Cox. Middle row: Lily Skidmore, -?-, Mary Peppy, Betty Flux, June Marks, Betty Peppy, Betty Close , -?-, -?-. The names of the three girls in the front row are not known.

Six
Trade and Industry

The water pump use for drilling coal bore holes in the field at the bottom of Winterbourne Hill. The workers are, left to right: Mr Ray Snr, Fred Tilley, Billy Ray, Duncan Smith. Below the Pennant stone lie coal measures by these have never been worked in the Winterbourne area. Between December 1915 and December 1917 a trial boring was made to a deapth of 2,338ft in the low ground near the viaduct spanning the Bristol to Iron Acton road but findings were only of very thin seams and did not justify commercial exploitation.

The Waterworks in Frampton Cotterell. These were situated on the site of former iron mines which operated from 1862 to 1874 when they closed due to severe flooding. In 1886 Frampton Cotterell drew its first piped supply from the 250,000 gallons of water hitherto running to waste each day while local wells, often polluted by sewage in times of heavy rain, were sources of typhoid and diphtheria. The West Gloucestershire Water Company continued in existence until 1958 when it was taken over by the Bristol Waterworks Company.

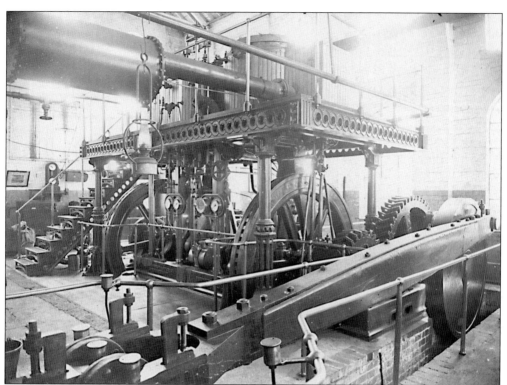

Waterworks machinery photographed by the late Mr George Watkins, c. 1936. The equipment consisted of two steam sets, one of which was housed in the tall red brick building (shown on the top of p. 90). A record exists in the archives of Messrs Gimson of Leicester of a pair of single cylinder engines being supplied to the West Gloucestershire Waterworks but unfortunately the entry is undated and does not make clear that they were to be used at Frampton Cotterell.

Mr C.W.A. Bowyer by the Easton pumping machine at the waterworks in 1926.

Waterworks staff, c. 1900. This photograph was taken at the time of the installation of new pumping machinery. The three men at the left of the back row and also the sixth in that row were all members of the Hanks family, involved for many years with the operation of the works. The little bearded man with the cap, sitting on the wall, was called Johnson and was affectionately known locally as 'Dr Johnson', a tribute to his skill in preparing herbal remedies. The overcoated man in the bowler hat next to Johnson was a Mr Andrews, Works Manager at the time.

Two views of the hat factory, Frampton Cotterell. Between 1818 and 1823, a factory was erected by Messrs Christy of Bermondsey in the three storey buildings in Park Lane. Firstly the work consisted of coagulating wool fibres and rabbit fur, a task which it was necessary to carry out in small, essentially unventilated cubicles on both sides of the workplace, each separated from its neighbour by a wooden partition. Inhalation of the flying fibres caused congestion of the lungs. Then followed a process of dipping the single pieces of composite fabric into a large cauldron of hot water containing sulphuric acid. The fumes arising from that process could have a debilitating effect on the mental health of the worker possibly explaining the origin of the phrase 'mad as a hatter'. By 1834 there were 120 people employed here producing about 110 dozen hats per week. However, in 1865 Christys introduced fur-cutting machinery which provoked a strike and eventually led, around 1870, to the concentration of the production in the firm's Stockport factory, whither some local families moved. The last independent hatter worked in the village in the first years of the twentieth century.

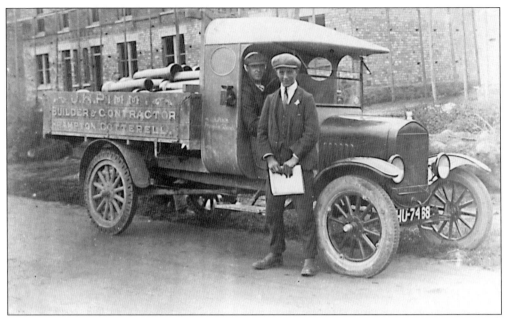

The Pimms (J. Hallett and Leonard R.) moved into Frampton Cotterell from London towards the end of the First World War. At first they occupied a house in Mill Lane but later moved to Winterbourne next door to what is now Jones' Garage. It would appear from the upper photograph that some of their work was concerned with local council house building.

The Skinner family who bought the former hat factory and adjoining workshops in 1876 set up a business which eventually came to include carpentry, building, wheelwrighting, painting and decoration and undertaking. Despite their varied skills they were slow in modernizing their own household facilities. This photograph is of young Margaret Skinner, granddaughter of the original proprietor, drawing water from the pump which was still in use in 1931.

By 1920 John Roland had given twenty-six years service to the then Frampton Cotterell Co-Operative and District Society which had its beginnings in 1894 during a period of labour unrest and poverty in the area. Many of the promoters were worshippers at the Primitive Methodist chapel on The Ridge.

The Frampton Cotterell and District Co-operative Society operated a butcher's shop subsequently taken over by the Bristol Co-op. It stood directly opposite the present Londis shop in Woodend Road. The uniformed, neatly coiffed and stiff-collared assistants in the photograph suggest a date of sometime just before the First World War. Note the artistic but precarious display arrangements of canned goods.

The Frampton Cotterell Co-operative Society became a limited company in 1915 and shortly afterwards opened these premises in Woodend Road with the manager's house to the right of the shop (just visible in the picture) and a meeting hall behind. In 1937 it became part of the Bristol Co-operative Society.

The Co-op in later years with the manager's house to the right. The curtained windows of the shop were those of the drapery department. All of the top floor was given over to committee rooms. Today it is the local Londis shop.

This scene shows the former post office in Church Road, Frampton Cotterell, which was in use until the late 1930s. The premises are now occupied by Keller and Co., accountants.

The present post office (right) pictured in 1906 when it seems to have served as a grocer's shop. The shuttered upper storey suggests possible use as a store for agricultural produce. It is interesting to note that the telephone system was in place so early in the century. The road surface looks in pretty poor condition.

The windmill in Ryecroft Road is a prominent Frampton Cotterell landmark. It was built by a member of the Pocock family in about 1825 and continued in use for some forty years. The building has lost approximately 15ft in height over the years. The adjacent chimney stack about 40ft high was used as the flue for a steam engine to power the mill when the wind dropped.

A 1910 view of the windmill showing Mr W.C. Milsom with his wagonette. The three girls are members of the Walters family who lived in the cottage part which is visible to the left of the photograph.

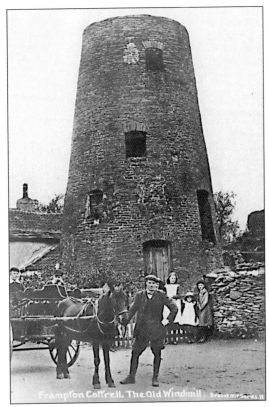

The Mill, Mill Lane, which is thought to have been built on the site of one of two earlier mills known to exist in the village in 1309. Seen here are the remnants of a complex of structures erected possibly during the 1820s. This included not only the mill but also a brewery, bakehouse, malthouse and fishery. Milling operations ceased just before the First World War and some ten years later the industrial buildings were demolished though the residential area became the headquarters of a haulage business run by Mr Albert Cook until 1960.

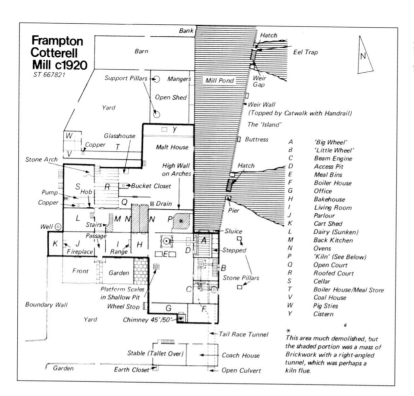

Frampton Cotterell Mill c1920
ST 667821

Bank

Barn

Support Pillars — Mangers

Open Shed

Yard

Glasshouse

W
V
Copper   T

Stone Arch

Pump
Copper

Well

S   Hob
R   Bucket Closet
Q   Drain

L   M N   N P *
Stairs
Passage
K   J   I   H
Fireplace   Range

Front   Garden

Platform Scales
in Shallow Pit
Boundary Wall   Wheel Stop

Yard   Chimney 45'/50'

Stable (Tallet Over)

Garden   Earth Closet

Malt House

High Wall
on Arches

Y

Mill Pond

Hatch

Eel Trap

Weir
Gap

Weir Wall
(Topped by Catwalk with Handrail)
The 'Island'

Buttress

Hatch

Pier

Sluice

Stepped

Stone Pillars

A
B
C
D
E
G   F

Tail Race Tunnel

Coach House

Open Culvert

N

A   'Big Wheel'
B   'Little Wheel'
C   Beam Engine
D   Access Pit
E   Meal Bins
F   Boiler House
G   Office
H   Bakehouse
I   Living Room
J   Parlour
K   Cart Shed
L   Dairy (Sunken)
M   Back Kitchen
N   Ovens
P   'Kiln' (See Below)
Q   Open Court
R   Roofed Court
S   Cellar
T   Boiler House/Meal Store
V   Coal House
W   Pig Sties
Y   Cistern

*
This area much demolished, but
the shaded portion was a mass of
Brickwork with a right-angled
tunnel, which was perhaps a
kiln flue.

A plan of the mill
buildings dating
from around 1920.

Frog Lane Pit, Coalpit Heath, *c.* 1905. A remarkable collection of other photographs of the colliery appears in John Cornwell's *Collieries of Kingswood and South Gloucestershire*. Iron mining also took place in Frampton Cotterell from 1864 to 1878 but no surviving photographs of this industry can be traced.

The winding house which was built in 1884.

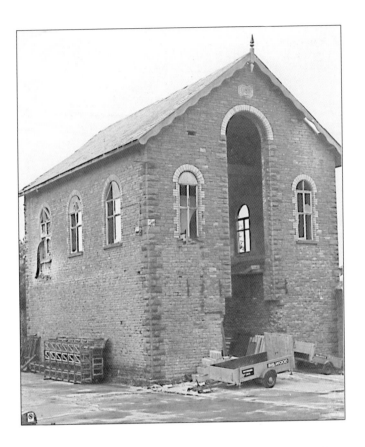

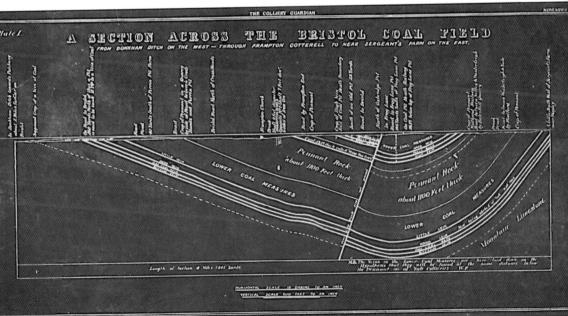

A cross section of the Bristol coalfield, published in the *Colliery Guardian*, 13 November 1874. The line of the coalface runs along Church Road.

Heathfield (later Heath Cottage), Coalpit Heath, was once occupied by Mr Robinson the colliery manager.

A delivery van outside the Half Moon pub, c. 1929. The petrol pump indicates how the pub adapted to the age of the motor just as the steps seen in the photograph on the top of p. 104 betray an earlier accommodation to equestrian traffic.

Mr George T. Stone ran a haulage service in addition to his responsibilities as pub landlord of the Half Moon Inn in Coalpit Heath. This photograph was taken around 1950.

A saddler's shop next to the Half Moon, Coalpit Heath. Apparently they also dealt in second hand iron goods and proprietary veterinary medicines.

Another view of the old inn. It was valued at £10 in the probate inventory of Thomas Price, a Westerleigh coal miner in 1736. This picture shows the old inn sign of a crescent moon with the profile of a man inside it. Local farm labourers appear in the working attire and the soldier's uniform suggests a date sometime during the First World War.

Roasting an ox behind the Half Moon on 3 May 1930. It took nearly twelve hours before the first slice could be served. The event was supervised by 'Mr F. Tyler, champion ox roaster of England' supported by the Stone brothers, George and Fred. The event attracted a large crowd swelled by the curious from outlying districts. The proceeds went to Chipping Sodbury Cottage Hospital.

The Ring of Bells, Coalpit Heath. This pub is believed to be of seventeenth-century origin. The tall chimney on the left suggests that beer was brewed on the premises when this picture was taken around 1900. In 1837 the pub was the headquarters of a miners' funeral club, a scheme which merged in 1873, with the colliers' doctor's fund started by the local branch of the miners' trade union.

The first Coalpit Heath post office situated in Back Lane. The Varlow family first came into the district from Iron Acton early in the nineteenth century. One of them was a carpenter. Another is later recorded as an 'engineer' (most likely a general maintenance man) in the service of the colliery and one of his sons was a local automobile engineer in the 1920s. The succession illustrates how one family can adapt to the changing situation brought about by technical innovation. The name 'Varlow' originates from Shropshire.

The remains of the Ram Hill pit. Raising coal at the Ram Hill pit was originally carried out by a horse-gin, a form of windlass or drum. A horse treading a circular path drew up tubs on a metal rope fixed to the drum. The pit shaft was situated in the garden immediately behind the sapling trees and was around 560ft deep. The site was abandoned by the late 1860s.

The terminus of the 'dram road' at the top of Ram Hill behind Walnut Cottage. The Ram Hill pit, the northernmost of the collieries, was situated here and by 1835 was able to send through traffic of loaded wagons to wharves on the Avon at Keynsham.

The footwear shop which stood next to The Mason's Arms, Watley's End. At one time it was owned by Mr Frank Howell and later by Mr William Chappell.

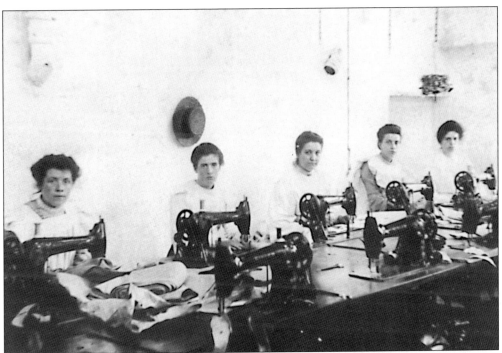

Machinists pictured in what was once the hat factory in Factory Road, Watley's End. When it was Todd's Clothing where trousers were made. There were always between twelve and twenty girls employed there and use was also made of outworkers. In 1926 a shilling could be earned for each pair of trousers completed.

Today's view of the old factory, now coverted into a garage.

The last day at The Old Brewery, Watley's End. Pictured here are the Thynne family with staff and friends. This building had served as a pub for over 200 years and had always been in the hands of two distantly related families: the Flooks and the Thynnes. In the cellar the name of S.F. Flook was found inscribed with the date 1855 and in Kelly's Directory for 1870 Mrs Pheobe Flook is listed as 'beer retailer and furrier'. Other owners were Abraham, Isacc and Alice Flook in the latter part of the nineteenth century. One daughter held fifty-six licences (i.e. she was landlady for fifty-six years). In 1940 it was taken over by Edgar Thynne who, after twenty years, passed it on to his son Gilbert. The inn finally closed its doors on 4 April 1964 and Gilbert Thynne became landlord of the nearby Mason's Arms.

Camp Quarry was on the other side of the River Frome. The bicycles could be from the early 1900s.

Quarry workers employed by George Bryant in Watley's End Road.

The photograph shows more workers and part of a lifting hoist. The picture was printed from a glass plate which was damaged.

The village shop in Watley's End Road when it was a general stores. Owned by Mrs Adams in 1912, it passed to Mr Dan Elliot in 1920 and then to a Miss Whiting. It later became a hairdressing salon but has now closed.

Maggs' shop, Watley's End. This business had been in Maggs' family since 1920 when it was run by Frank Maggs who doubled up as a postman. His daughter Mrs Marion Lowe was next in line and was succeeded by Donald Maggs. The last owner was Richard Maggs who was forced to give up through ill health. Were they, perhaps, descended from Robert Maggs, he that was listed as a hat manufacturer in 1870?

The George and Dragon at the end of the High Street, Winterbourne, where the first school was held in 1813, a temporary arrangement while Bourne House was being built. The landlady at that time was a Mrs Elizabeth Maggs. There was a Maggs occupying the inn as far back as 1786.

WINTERBOURNE, NEAR BRISTOL.   No. 407.

The Wheatsheaf in the High Street, Winterbourne, and a traffic-free scene as children pose for the camera. Could the gentleman in the pub doorway be James Dance, the landlord?

Another view of the Wheatsheaf with a military man cycling by. On the far right was a general stores run by Annie Dando. The white cottages and the shop were demolished to make space for a pub car park. The woman in a long dark skirt and light blouse in the distance stands outside the post office which was run by the Ludwell family for sixty-eight years until its closure in early 1971.

'Sunset View' was built by Mr Hughland in 1928 on land that was previously a market garden and smallholding. It was also known as Beggar's Rest as the old sheds were used by tramps and beggars. The house has since been renamed 'Tree Tops' and is used for bed and breakfast.

The last cottage on the left in this picture incorporated a shop and garage selling radios and cycles. The proprietor was a man called Alex Jones who lived to be ninety-seven. He died in 1997. On the far right were other shops, a boot and shoe store, a newsagents run by Sally Pritchard, and a grocery store owned, in turn, by the Elliots, the Langdons and the Ampletts who took over in 1942 and stayed until the final closure in 1962.

The last shop in the rank was run by Mrs Billingham with the assistance of Mrs Skidmore who lived across the road. This shop was pulled down to widen Nicholls Lane.

Down farmhouse, possibly seen in the 1930s. Built in 1826, it was owned by the Matthews family from 1860 to 1950 and then by Dr H.L. O'Sullivan. It was later pulled down and a new block of flats was built on the site.

A fine sketch of the Royal Oak inn, Winterbourne, when it contained only one room. It now incorporates three more cottages.

The general stores in Winterbourne when it was owned by T.H. Grove who sold haberdashery, groceries and beer.

The same shop, when it was in the hands of the Draisey family who added house furnishings and petrol to their range of goods. The shop is now owned by the Harris family who can still offer competitive prices.

The Draiseys provided a door-to-door service.

The first bus to go into service at Winterbourne, registration no. AE 731. It was registered on 6 December 1913 and was a Bristol C65 built by Bristol Tramways. It was a twenty-eight-seater.

A Hepworth's picture taken from Worrall's Lane, Winterbourne Down in the 1920s, after the village hall was built in 1921. Worrall's Lane seems to have been named for George Worrall who, in 1827, owned nearby Waterpark Farm. The hall, which closed about 1953, was given to the village together with land by the daughters of the first vicar, Revd F.W. Greenstreet.

OLD MILL, WINTERBOURNE DOWN

A view of the Old Mill at Winterbourne Down, looking across the old stone bridge which was washed away in the 1968 floods. In 1827 it was known as 'Jones' Mill'. The Kelly's Directory of 1870 gives the information that Robert Jones was the owner. It was later sold to a Mr England who continued to run it as a corn mill and in later years it was used as a cider press. The water wheel was 15ft in diameter and 6ft broad. The mill closed in the mid-1920s.

The horse and carts belong to Thomas Free, a local quarry owner from Frenchay. Behind Winterbourne Mill was a quarry run by the England family.

Quarry workers at G. England and Sons in Winterbourne Down. Their main trade was flag and kerb stones. In 1896 Ernest Cox began work here as an apprentice for three shillings a week which rose to five shillings by 1898. The following year he had an increase of two shillings and by 1900 was taking home ten shillings weekly. Under the terms of his apprenticeship he was forbidden to marry, gamble, play cards or dice, drink or sell his master's goods. This picture was taken in 1920 and shows, left to right, seated in the centre: Ernest Cox, Brusher Maggs, Aaron England (with hammer). On the far right is one of the Englands and next to him Isaac Cordy. They are all wearing hats or caps and mufflers.

Some of the same workers with the crane that was in use in the background. Note the deep clefts that have been cut.

Winterbourn Down post office as it was in 1910 with Mrs Ford the postmistress standing outside. Prior to Mrs Ford it was run by Mrs Bird and afterwards by Mrs Mann, followed by Mrs Clarke, Mrs Marshall, Mrs Casewell and Mrs Carter. The present postmistress is Mrs Mona Parker who takes a great interest in village life.

The main shop in Winterbourne Down for many years. Apart from serving as a grocery and drapery store it also incorporated a bakery.

Seven

The Railway

Cutting out the rock between Mill Road and Winterbourne station.

Building the viaduct. Note the carrier on top of the rails.

A similar scene but taken from the other side. Coils of rope can be observed on the fence posts and a long ladder on the third buttress.

This is thought to be the bridge at Coalpit Heath the clue lying in the telegraph posts. A steam crane can be seen also the ladders needed for reaching the full height.

Coalpit Heath station and staff. Note the luggage trolley in the foreground and the sign indicating a separate 'ladies' waiting room on the right. In 1922 there were five trains a day to Bristol, three of which came from London. Because they stopped at every station the journey took nearly four hours. Two trains came through from Swindon. The frequency of service was the same in the opposite direction with the addition of one train to Chipping Sodbury. In 1938 the services were the same but there were two additional trains on Saturdays to and from Little Somerford, the junction for Malmesbury, and Hullavington. The station had no Sunday service and closed on 3 April 1961.

Workers laying the line.

Laying sleepers for trolleys to cross the line at the end of Winterbourne station. Two names are known: fourth from left is Jack Adams and the ganger with the double watch chain is Ernie Simmonds.

More workers pause to pose for the camera. Second left, back row is Bob Anstey.

Here the men are laying ballast between the sleepers.

Building the station master's house at Coalpit Heath. All such dwellings were built in a similar style. The ornamental ledge running between the two floors seems to have been a popular feature. The fence, which is in the process of being erected in this picture, still stands today.

Winterbourne workers pictured on the occasion of being awarded a prize for the best kept section of track in 1932. Left to right, standing: Alfie Clark, Reg Hares, George Flook, Jim Woodbury. In the front: Albert Bisp, Harry Skidmore, Albert Andrews, Bill Dixon.

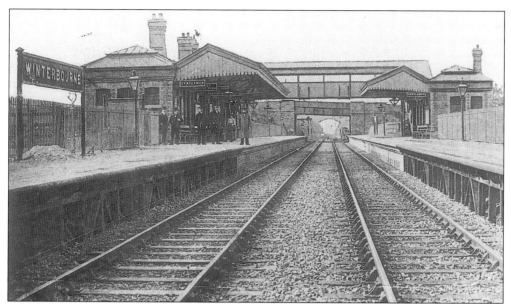

Winterbourne station. Although it was always a busier station than Coalpit Heath, Winterbourne had its initial complement of eight staff in 1903 which was halved by 1930. Over 13,000 tickets were issued 1903 and more than another 10,000 ten years later. It closed on the same day as Coalpit Heath on 3 April 1961. However the railway tradition did not die overnight. A group of workmen who came to occupy a hut on the former platform exhibited a sheet informing visitors of their unavailability during lunch hours '1 to 2pm SX'.

A long range view of Winterbourne station.

Huckford quarry with Winterbourne station in the background.

The only female porter ever to work at Winterbourne station – Miss Gladys Maggs.